THE GREAT

CANADIAN NORTHWEST

RAIL PICTORIAL

by

J. Edward Martin

STUDIO E

British Columbia, Canada

Canadian Cataloguing in Publication Data

Martin, J. Edward.
  The great Canadian Northwest rail pictorial

  ISBN 0-920716-04-0

  1. Railroads--Canada, Western--History. 2. Railroads--
Canada, Western--History--Pictorial works. I. Title.
HE2808.M36 1995   385'.09712   C95-910283-3

Cover: White Pass & Yukon #73 at Carcross (author's photo, 1982)

Printed in Canada

ISBN 920716-04-0

CONTENTS

The Train Watchers, Edmonton

INTRODUCTION

From their very beginning in the 1800s, railways have fascinated people of all ages, worldwide. The excitement, the special sounds, the irresistible appeal to the imagination has generated legions of train enthusiasts, inspired countless pictures and writings. In the following photographic essay, the reader is invited to sample some of the railway delights of the Canadian Northwest (that vast expanse from the head of the Great Lakes to the Pacific and the Arctic) and to revel in their absorbing history.

In 1883, when the first shipment of western grain to eastern Canada left Fort William aboard the lakeboat *Erin*, it marked the beginning of a great saga. Whereas shovels and wheelbarrows were used at the start, grain as well as coal, sulphur, potash and many other commodities came to be emptied mechanically by the carload and transferred on giant conveyors. The trains themselves likewise changed, growing from about a dozen cars to around a hundred apiece. Indeed, the scale of operations became Herculean, with millions of metric tonnes moved with ever-increasing rapidity.

It may be noticed that the first chapter is devoted to the Canadian Pacific Railway. Its importance to the country historically should not be under-valued. As the first transcontinental, the CPR tied Canada together, opened up the western plains to settlement and ensured that the Northwest would remain connected to the British crown. The company's specialized equipment, its tunnels and other engineering achievements are also of great significance and they too merit considerable attention. At the same time, however, it must be remembered that the Canadian Pacific was not the only railway to contribute to the total result, nor was it the first. Locomotives were hauling coal on Vancouver Island twenty-two years before the last spike was driven on the CPR and building the other railways was often just as important as construction of the Canadian Pacific.

Of perennial interest and visually very evident in the following pages, is the American influence on Canadian railways. The reader will find many similarities in the buildings and equipment of the two countries but so too will differences in design and practice be evident. While a large number of railway builders and supplies did come from the United States, the rigorous Canadian climate made special demands that could not be ignored.

Changes in railway technology over the years have substantially altered the railways' appearance. Foremost and perhaps the most apparent was the conversion from steam to diesel locomotion. Water tanks, which once stood at fifty-mile intervals, vanished. Coaling towers, turntables and roundhouses at each division point disappeared. Other, quite independent developments also took effect at about the same time. Motorized scooters, capable of patrolling forty miles of track every forty-eight hours eliminated most section houses. Before 1960, gangs of about four men went over only six to twelve mile sections of track and those gangs generally required railway housing. Small railway stations likewise largely disappeared, not just because passenger trains declined but because new technology, in the form of satellites and microwave radio, made their abandonment possible.

Unchanged in the story is Nature and railways continue to grapple with it, in all its forms. Radio has speeded reaction to forest and grass fires and helicopter patrols are now able to find and rectify beaver-caused flooding but wind and snow still test the skill of railway engineers. Much has been done to reduce washouts and avalanches but the day of completely uninterrupted rail service has not yet arrived.

Relations with the natural world have improved considerably. Like its American cousins, the CPR in its early days advertised the abundance of wildlife along its lines available for massacre. Animals were even shot from moving trains, not from need or self-defense but simply for killing's sake. Railways of to-day are much more ecology minded, much more sensitive to the needs of the other species. Not long ago, for instance, when wild Canada geese built their nest between the ties of a railway bridge on the CPR's Empress Subdivision, in Saskatchewan, the birds were neither forcibly evicted, nor molested in any way. Instead, trains were ordered to exercise extreme caution in passing. The goslings hatched and the performance was repeated several years in a row. Other evidences of a new era of enlightenment include linemen in the Banff area building platforms on the tops of poles for nesting osprey and hot steam being substituted for herbicides to control weed growth along the tracks.

Lastly, before plunging into the body of the book, it should be noted that the railways of the Northwest must not be taken for granted. Their existence in the years to come is not at all guaranteed. Government-financed and maintained roads and airports have already effectively destroyed rail passenger service in Canada. Rubber-tired freight trains (multiple-trailer trucks) now fill the highways, eroding further the breadth of railway sources of revenue. Canadian governments as a whole have failed to understand that railways are by far the most economical, the most energy-efficient, the most rational and most environmentally friendly means of transportation. Financial support for upgrading, in the form of electrification and high-speed passenger and freight trains, has been almost non-existent. There has not been the realization that the diesel-electric locomotive is outmoded technology of the early 20th century, incapable of permitting Canada or its railways to compete adequately in the 21st. It can only be hoped that the full importance of rail transportation to the economy and the well-being of Canadians will be realized in time and that the necessary steps will be taken to ensure railway survival and improvement.

THE CANADIAN PACIFIC RAILWAY

Driving the Last Spike on the CPR

In this, perhaps the most famous picture in Canadian railway history, Donald A. Smith not only marks the completion of the Canadian Pacific Railway, as he drives the ceremonial Last Spike, on 7 November 1885. He is in effect tying together the Canadian nation. Smith (later Lord Strathcona) was a senior director of the CPR. Behind him, with top hat and equally white beard is Sandford Fleming, original engineer-in-chief for the Pacific Railway. Fleming was also a CPR director for thirty years but is better known for his accepted system of world time. Further to the left, with clipped black whiskers, is William C. Van Horne, then general manager but later president of the railway, succeeding George Stephen in 1888. It was thrifty Van Horne who decreed that an ordinary iron track spike be used for the ceremony and that everyone wishing to go to see it would have to pay full fare. His famous short speech for the occasion: "All I can say is that the work has been well done, in every way" could certainly not have been more economizing either. At right, on the two crossties connecting roadbed from the East and West is Major A.B. Rogers, finder of the mountain pass that made the event possible here, at Craigellachie, in Eagle Pass (about 28 miles west of Revelstoke) instead of the Yellowhead. Most noticeably absent in the picture is an indication of how many workers the job had taken. Andrew Onderdonk, the western end's contractor had brought in 65,000 Chinese alone.

The First Transcontinental Passenger Train Arrives

    The first regularly scheduled CPR passenger train, the "Pacific Express," arrives in Port Moody, BC, exactly at noon, on 4 July 1886. It had left Montreal's Dalhousie Square Station on the evening of 28 June, with a ten-car consist of four sleepers, the dining car "Holyrood," two coaches, three baggage and mail cars. By the time it arrived at Port Moody, only five remained, as cars were dropped and changed en route. Its locomotive had been changed twenty-six times and although flags, bunting and evergreen boughs decorated some of the engines, #371 came to a halt in front of the west coast station unadorned, looking very business-like.

    The 4-4-0 had rolled out of the CPR's New Shops in Montreal just three months before and it would work until being scrapped, in October 1915. Only one of the coaches, official car #78, added to the train at North Bend, has been preserved. After being retired from service in 1960, it was given to the Canadian Railway Museum, near Montreal. As for the dockside Port Moody station, it was replaced by another wooden depot situated about a half mile closer to the centre of town, in 1908. The 1886 station was then sold to an oil company and used for offices, before being demolished in 1961. Only its brass chandelier was salvaged, for display at City Hall.

    As a footnote, it may be added that the 1908 station was moved in 1945, by cutting it in half and sliding it on greased rails a half mile further into town, pulled by a yard engine. That depot is now a museum.

CPR Freight Train at Little Pic River, Ontario

Boxcars and flats with road trailers riding "piggyback" round the big bend at Little Pic, behind a pair of humming Canadian Pacific diesels. It is August, 1965 and many years have passed since the first trackbuilding crews of the CPR wrestled with the patience-testing natural elements of this region north of Lake Superior. A portion of the almost 32,000 square mile lake, the largest in the world, may be seen in the upper left.

Cost of building this scenic but rugged section of line, which provided an all-Canadian rail connection between East and West, was enormous. Soggy muskeg had swallowed both track and equipment overnight. Hordes of mosquitos and flies had made life miserable for workers in the summer and the winter was unbearably cold. Millions of cubic feet of rock had to be moved but the Canadian Shield was conquered and traversed, in 1884. On 31 October 1885, the Canadian Pacific Western Division could announce in the Winnipeg Free Press that "The New All-Rail Line to the East is now open through Canadian Territory. Commencing Sunday 1 November, through trains will leave Winnipeg daily except Saturdays at 8 p.m. for Port Arthur, Ottawa, Toronto, Montreal and all points East."

Early Canadian Pacific Station at Revelstoke, B.C.

Wearing black sleeve protectors, Revelstoke's station agent and telegraph operator strike impressive poses at the waiting room door, in the early 1890s. From the telegraph bay extends the lantern-topped arm of a flattened oval Order Board in the "no orders" position. Others on the typical wooden station platform may be waiting passengers, travelling salesmen, railway men, or simply lounging townspeople, for the railway station was the centre of both cultural and economic activity in virtually every western Canadian town, for decades.

Replacing the initial, temporary tent or modified boxcar depots, were wooden stations built to standard designs. The one used at Revelstoke was one of the first and most commonly used on the CPR, a type found from Ontario to the west coast. There was no overhanging roof or canopy and decoration was sparse, more or less limited to diagonal sheathing and a little coping saw work in the band separating the two storeys. A waiting room was placed on one side of the office, with a freight room set on the other. Upstairs were living quarters for the station agent and his family, a feature more prevalent in Canada than in the United States.

Revelstoke at the time of this photo obviously had not the importance as a rail centre, that it would later have. In 1898, it became divisional point for the line between Lake Louise and Kamloops, replacing Donald. At that time, Revelstoke gained rail shops and a roundhouse.

The Vancouver Terminal of 1898

    Because Port Moody was too hemmed in by a steep hillside, somewhat limiting available harbour and rail yard space, the western terminus for the Canadian Pacific Railway was moved to Vancouver, in May 1887. At first, a tiny, wooden shed known as "Hastings" served as its station, for Vancouver was little more than a forest but in 1898 the fine, mottled brick and stone structure with slate roofs shown above replaced it, at the foot of Granville Street. Company offices were located in the floors above the ticket and waiting room areas. Designed by Montreal architect Edward Maxwell, the massive chateau-styled building celebrated the brilliant success of the railway. Unfortunately, the structure seems to have had design flaws, for it was replaced by another brick and steel station directly to the right of it, in 1914.

    At least two of Canadian Pacific's white Empress ocean liners can be seen in the background, along with several other smaller craft docked nearby. The railway had gotten into the shipping business in 1884, when its first passenger/cargo steamers were placed in service out of Owen Sound, Ontario. On the Pacific coast, the CPR began by chartering a sailing ship, the W.B. Flint, which arrived at Port Moody with cargo in July, 1886. The CPR's own Pacific fleet was begun with the launching, in Britain, of the steamship "Empress of India," in January 1891. It sailed for Vancouver on 7 February that same year and the "Empress of Japan" and the "Empress of China" followed a few months later.

The Old Log Station at Banff, ca.1890

Above: *To harmonize fully with Banff's natural beauty, the CPR built this special station of round, peeled logs, in 1886. After the railway opened its Banff Springs Hotel in June 1888, carriages like the small, open one seen backed up to the platform provided taxi service between the two.*

Left: *One of four wooden, caboose-like observation cars of 1902, built to supplement a trio of open-top coaches, in service in the scenic Rockies since 1890.*

The Canadian at Banff

Diesel-electric locomotive #1416 arrives in Banff, Alberta, with the world famous "Canadian," eastbound to Montreal, in early May, 1971. To the left in the picture, almost lost in the deep shadow of its roof's great overhang, is the fieldstone and stucco station that in 1910 replaced the log structure seen on the opposite page.

The Canadian began in 1953, with the purchase of 173 new, stainless steel cars from the American coach builder, Budd. These were designed to provide the best in travel comfort and the Canadian would soon take precedence over all other trains on the system. Unlike the all-sleeper transcontinental of old, it offered both coach and sleeper accommodation. There was a dining car as well as roomettes and travellers were treated to air-conditioning, something almost indispensable in the many glass domes. The first "Canadians" left Toronto and Montreal on 24 April 1955. Only three nights, instead of four, were now required for the transcontinental trip to Vancouver. Average speed was just over 40 miles per hour, about 7 mph faster than predecessors. The trains enjoyed good patronage right to the end of their existence and when VIA, which took them over in September 1978, dropped service over the Vancouver-Calgary-Winnipeg line in mid-January 1990, following Conservative government cuts in support, there was widespread sadness and indignation.

The Rogers Pass

Beneath the snowy peaks of the Selkirks, the small frame station in Rogers Pass quietly awaits an approaching train, the natural silence disturbed only by the locomotive's bell and whistle.

Early in 1881, the CPR hired an American ex-soldier, Major Albert Bowman Rogers, to find a way through the Selkirk Range much further south than the Yellowhead Pass, which Sandford Fleming had charted. After months of arduous trekking through steep, tangled forest, the objective was finally glimpsed but confirmation and announcement came only the next August.

Construction crews reached the summit (altitude 4,275 feet, or 1,330 metres) on 17 August 1885 and trains began to move through toward Revelstoke. The worst of all was yet to come, however. The first year, 40 feet (12 metres) of snow landed on the track in places and rail traffic ground to a halt. Rock slides and avalanches would plague operation of the railway for many years to come. Although thirty-one snowsheds were built, totaling over 6 kilometres in length, disasters did not cease. Between 1885 and 1911, over 200 men were killed by slides. Seven lives were lost on 31 January 1899, when the station shown above, along with its water tower and roundhouse, were suddenly smashed and buried. After the five mile long Connaught Tunnel, 554 feet (168 m) below the summit, opened for traffic on 13 December 1916, the dangerous surface route was abandoned. A longer, 9.1 mile (14.7 km.) tunnel completed in 1988, took the line another 360 feet (109 m) lower still.

14

Steam Locomotives for the Mountains

*In the West, the Canadian Pacific quickly found that it needed much more powerful locomotives than those employed in the East. The standard 4-4-0 American type (a four-wheeled lead truck followed by four driving wheels and none trailing) could supply neither the power, nor the adhesion necessary for climbing mountains with heavy trains. Even engines with six, or eight driving wheels had difficulty. An eight-car passenger train required three such locomotives to conquer the 4.4% grades on the Big Hill, near Field, B.C. Freight trains needed four. Spiral tunnels in the nearby Kicking Horse Pass cut the ruling grade in half, in September 1909 but with increasingly heavier trains, stronger locomotives were still needed. **Above, #1950,** a Mallet type, with opposed cylinders and an articulated frame. It operated much like a pair of ballroom dancers, one set of wheels going forward, while the other was in reverse. It was one of six built in CPR's Angus Shops, in 1905 and 1912. They were later converted to conventional 2-10-0s, joining Decapods such as **#5790, below,** built by the CPR in 1917-19. All of them remained in service until the 1950s, some used as yard engines on the Prairies. From these developed the slightly larger 2-10-4 Selkirk type, built from 1929 to 1949.*

Westbound CPR Grain Train in the Rockies

Under a late September sun, a trio of colorful General Motors SD 40-2 diesels rumble westward through the Rockies to the coast in 1981, hauling a long, solid train of prairie grain cars. The use of steam engines on the CPR had ceased in 1960 and thereafter they would be seen only for special excursions.

Diesels do not have to be fueled and watered so often as steam locomotives. No turntables, no firemen are required and runs can be greatly extended before change of engines or crew is necessary. Units run harmoniously in multiples, all controlled from the lead locomotive. Given these very considerable economies, the diesel-electric's speedy replacement of steam in the 1950s is perfectly understandable, financially.

The SD 40-2 gained great popularity on the railway in the 1970s and 80s. Its six powered axles gave excellent traction and the 3,000 horsepower units were found both versatile and capable of pulling heavy loads, at speeds over 60 mph.

Canadian Pacific, after testing radio remote control of mid-train and rear "robot" units in 1967, put the system into widespread use. It was especially useful for long, 100-car trains of coal, grain and other bulk items in the Canadian West. Something of a record was set in November, 1974. Using seven diesels, 252 cars carrying 19,858 tons of grain were moved to Thunder Bay in a single train almost 2½ miles (6 kilometres) long.

Medicine Hat Divisional Station With vast deposits of natural gas nearby, Medicine Hat quickly gained importance as a railroad centre. Locally manufactured goods and Lethbridge coal for CPR steam engines flowed through the Hat. After the CPR's purchase of North Western Coal & Navigation's railway in 1897, freight and passengers for the Crow's Nest Pass line increased traffic even further. The red brick station above is double its 1907 size.

CPR Swift Current, Saskatchewan Canadian Pacific's Prairie Region begins here, at Swift Current and runs over 5,500 miles (8,800 km) east to Thunder Bay, Ontario. The 4,750 mile (7,600 km) Pacific Region extends westward, to Port Alberni, B.C. Importance to the railway is implicit in the presence of the two, well-built brick station buildings beside the tracks.

The Wide Open Spaces

Above: *Wetaskiwin, Alta., in 1898, a typical Prairie town, with a false-fronted main street, wooden railway station and a big grain elevator. The CPR-owned Calgary & Edmonton Railway was laid quickly over these mostly flat grasslands, from Macleod to Strathcona, in 1891.*

Left: *Canadian Pacific's M-499, a 1930s Buick with flanged wheels and a cowcatcher, at the Western Development Museum, in Moose Jaw. It once served for area track inspection.*

Steam Locomotives for the Prairies

Eight driving wheels were often needed for climbing out of the Prairie's many deep river valleys. One 2-8-0 Consolidation type, has been preserved in Lethbridge. Another, CPR **#3716**, shown **above**, still pulls summer tourist trains, on the west coast. It was built in 1912, by Montreal Locomotive Works. The locomotive's fully-enclosed, "all-weather" cab became a Canadian standard feature, after first appearing on CPR 4-6-2 #1011, in March, 1911.

    Below, Streamlined CPR **#2911**, a 4-4-4 "Jubilee" type built by Canadian Locomotive Works, in Kingston Ontario, in 1937. The majority of this class was used in the West, for high speed passenger service out of Winnipeg, Moose Jaw, Regina and Calgary. Six Moose Jaw-Regina trains a day, for instance, were handled by Jubilees in the great days of steam.

The Louise Bridge, at Winnipeg

CP Rail's bright, red switcher #7035, a 1,000 horsepower Alco S2 built in 1945, pauses with a string of grain cars on the historic Louise Bridge at Winnipeg, in the Fall of 1981. A signals box, in fresh aluminum paint, can be seen by its side.

The massive, black steel truss bridge on which the train rests was built over the Red River by the City of Winnipeg in 1881, to ensure that the Canadian Pacific Railway expanded westward from there, rather than from Selkirk, to the North. The deal was further sweetened by the gift of land for right-of-way and a station, which remained tax-free until 1965. Sandford Fleming's plan had been to run the CPR west from Selkirk, crossing the narrows of Lake Manitoba, on its way to the Yellowhead Pass. The bridge-building was done just in time. William Van Horne's track construction crew of 5,000 men and 1,700 teams of horses set out the following Spring, bound for Portage La Prairie and Calgary.

Progress across the Prairies was swift. After a slow start hampered by Spring floods, Van Horne had the men laying an average of over three miles per day and up to six at the last. Problems with Indians along the route were minor, consisting of survey stakes being torn up, or threatening postures taken. Tactful handling by the Northwest Mounted Police and an Oblate missionary named Father Lacombe averted the bloody skirmishes so common south of the border. Calgary was reached on 13 August 1883.

The Lethbridge Viaduct

Above, a CPR train of gondola cars crosses the Oldman River valley at Lethbridge, on the highest, longest railway bridge in Canada. It is 314 feet high and 5,327 feet (over a mile) long. The project's engineer, John E. Schwitzer, was also designer of the spiral tunnels in Kicking Horse Pass.

Right: A travelling crane running on oak rails and high enough for railway cars to pass under it, lowers another section of one of the 33 riveted steel support towers into place, during construction of the viaduct. The first train crossed on 29 October 1909.

The Crowsnest

Above is Crows Nest station, with a ladder on its roof to use in case of fire, and the station agent's family and a section crew arrayed on the platform. Like all the other stations of this size and style (except the one from Elko, which has been moved to a railway museum in Cranbrook), it has long since disappeared. Around the turn of the century, however, when this photograph was taken, such depots were indispensable to the CPR, everywhere.

The Crowsnest line from Lethbridge to Kootenay Landing, near Nelson, BC opened on 18 June 1899. It had been built by the Canadian Pacific, using subsidies resulting from an agreement with the federal government two years earlier. Under that agreement, the railway received $11,000 per mile constructed but had to ship prairie grain to the lakehead at a rate fixed by the government. Political pressure extended the rate's application to the Canadian National Railways and to westbound grain in 1927. Shipments to Churchill, on Hudson's Bay, were added in 1931. The Crow Rate became a contentious issue between all parties, which did not cease until the Crow was abolished, on 1 January 1984.

The Crowsnest Pass line gave the Canadian Pacific relatively easy access to the mineral-rich Kootenays. It also made possible a faster Spokane to St. Paul service than the Great Northern could offer. A connection in Saskatchewan to the CP-controlled Soo Line and an extension from the Crowsnest line south, through Yahk and Kingsgate was used. Completion westward, via the Coquihalla Pass to Hope, in 1916 furnished the CPR with a second route to the Pacific.

Stations in the Kootenays   Situated on the Crowsnest line, about halfway between the Alberta/BC border and Nelson is this modern, International style station at Cranbrook. While under construction in 1945, on the site of an earlier depot dating to 1898, three boxcars served as a temporary station, following a tradition dating back to the first days of the railway.

Right: *The dormered, white junction depot at Castlegar, built in 1907. Surrounded by a triangle of rail lines, its placement is somewhat unique. One line leads northeast to Nelson and the Crowsnest, one goes south to Trail, the other west to Grand Forks. Shortly after this photo was taken in 1981, the station became a museum.*

Port Packer, Coquitlam

In keeping with the up-scaling so general in the last decades of the twentieth century, CP Rail in 1980 invested in giant, mobile container-handling machines like the one above, costing $350,000 apiece. Having a 75,000 pound (33,750 kg) capacity, they can easily lift large, 44-foot (13.2 metre) domestic containers. One is seen here in the monster's steel arms, at the railway's Mayfair terminal in Coquitlam, B.C. A special device enables the machine to also lift road trailers. Behind the packer are some of the flat cars specially designed for handling trailers and containers. Some are over 89 feet (26.7m) long and can handle up to four containers apiece.

Containers are now used for most freight shipment by both rail and sea. Merchandise is better protected from the elements and damage is reduced. Much handling is eliminated, speeding delivery and since the containers are waterproof and can be stacked outside, warehousing is not required. Door-to-door delivery can be easily made, using trucks.

The Canadian Pacific Railway Company decided to re-name itself "CP Rail" in 1968 and instituted the geometrical logo so lavishly displayed on all equipment in the picture above. The move reduced the tedium and expense of bilingual lettering and made a symbol instantly recognizable by even the illiterate.

Via Dayliner at Courtenay, B.C.

In bright sunshine, southbound passengers wait for those arriving to alight, before boarding the VIA dayliner at Courtenay, in October 1987. The 139-mile (224 km) journey from Victoria to Courtenay was made in four and a half hours.

VIA dayliner #6134 (ex-CPR #9065) is a stainless steel Budd RDC built in 1957, two years after self-propelled Rail Diesel Cars were first introduced on the Victoria-Courtenay run. The RDC offered reasonably fast, quiet, smooth and very comfortable transportation, with wide windows, soft seats and air-conditioning. The first of these cars in Canada was demonstrated on the CNR at Turcot, Quebec, in January 1951.

The Esquimalt & Nanaimo Railway was built by coal magnate Robert Dunsmuir and on 13 August 1886, Canadian Prime Minister John A. Macdonald drove the last spike in the line, at Cliffside (about 25 miles north of Victoria). The railway was bought by the Canadian Pacific in 1905, with the intention to continue it on to Campbell River. Rails were extended north from Parksville in 1914 but the Great War intervened and rails went no further than Courtenay.

The federal government's VIA Rail Corporation took over E&N passenger service and stations in 1978. Good scenery and points of interest along the line were not lacking. Nevertheless, only one, single car train a day each way was operated in the final years and in 1994, VIA was granted permission to abandon passenger service on Vancouver Island.

Vancouver Island Memories

Above, Pacific Coal Company's locomotive, the "San Francisco," sits at South Wellington, with a load from No.5 Mine. Alongside, the bearded, bowler-hatted engine driver stands with his typical, long-spouted oil can. When this photograph was taken in 1896, knuckle couplers (note the link type on the pilot beam) were not yet mandatory on industrial railways. Trains of Pacific Coal (another Dunsmuir enterprise), travelled only a short distance, for the Esquimalt & Nanaimo Railway was extended to Wellington in 1887.

Left, an E&N passenger train behind locomotive #2 steams into Nanaimo, about 1905. The depot in the picture burnt down and was replaced by a much larger stucco and shingle structure, in 1920.

26

The Roberts Bank Coal Terminal

Above, a large ocean freighter anchors at Roberts Bank, its hold filling with coal from huge conveyor belts. Behind it, a single CPR unit train circles the facility, on a great loop of track.

Following agreements made in 1968-69, to ship Kootenay coal to Japan, for use in that country's steel mills, a new deep-sea bulk terminal was constructed at Roberts Bank, 20 miles south of Vancouver. To carry coal to the coast in volume, unit trains of 98 bathtub gondolas were devised by Canadian Pacific, using the latest technology. They became a virtual conveyor, rarely broken and seldom stopped on the 1,400-mile round trip. Trains are unloaded automatically, moved by a mechanical, steel indexer through a rotary dumper that empties two cars at a time. All the while, the cars remain coupled together, thanks to special couplings. Since each gondola carries 105 tons of coal, several locomotives are required at the front, in the middle and sometimes on the rear. Before the Rogers Pass was given a new line with a maximum grade of only 1% in 1988, as many as twelve 3,000 hp diesels were required to move a loaded train through it.

The first CP Rail unit coal train arrived at Roberts Bank on 30 April 1970. Later, Canadian National and Burlington Northern also began to deliver there. While the National Harbours Board operated the track at first, it was turned over to BC Rail, in 1983.

The Royal Hudson

    The famous CPR Royal Hudson #2860 visits White Rock, B.C., to help celebrate that city's 25th anniversary, in April 1982. The celebrity has just been mobbed by enthusiastic admirers and now seeks some tranquility further along the Burlington Northern's line. It will return later to North Vancouver and the annual summer excursions to Squamish, which began in 1974.
    CPR #2860's running board crowns and "Royal" name recall sister engine #2850's assignment to haul the King and Queen's train, on their Canadian tour of 1939.

CANADIAN NATIONAL RAILWAYS

CNR Steam Locomotive #6060

On an overcast October day in 1973, Canadian National Railways locomotive #6060 waits on a siding at the Science Museum in Ottawa, while oil and water are replenished. The bullet-nosed beauty had returned to the rails for steam excursions, after sitting idle for years as a display piece in Jasper, Alberta.

The Montreal Locomotive Works product was built in 1944, for fast passenger service on the Montreal-Toronto run. It burned coal when it began life but when diesels taok over in the East in 1955, #6060 was converted to oil and sent West. When the CNR retired all of its steam power on 31 December 1960, most locomotives were scrapped, many of them no older than #6060. There were many miles left in her, however, and thus she was saved, exhibited and in 1972 refurbished. Following eight years in the East, she returned in 1980 to Edmonton, at which time the Alberta Government took her over. Apart from a trip to Vancouver's Expo in 1986, the locomotive then spent little time out of storage until 1992, when the Rocky Mountain Rail Society bought it for a dollar, with the intention of running it once again, in Alberta.

GTPR Track Gang, Stony Plain, Alberta

With hair neatly combed, a Grand Trunk Pacific track gang poses for a picture, about 1912. Behind the men on the left are milk cans, some probably filled with water for the hard-working crew. On the right a lone female, possibly cook for the gang, or the station operator's wife, sits on a hand-pumped three-wheel "speeder" used for basic transportation. In the foreground, a jack is in position, ready to raise rail for levelling the track. The Grand Trunk Pacific Railway prided itself on smooth, well-laid line, better than the Canadian Northern's, which ran parallel to it for many miles west from Edmonton to the Yellowhead Pass. GTPR newspaper ads of 1914 unabashedly shouted "Travel Via The Best Railroad Ever Constructed."

The turreted, wooden station is a Standard Design A, the most common of the GTPR. Approximately 300 of them were built to plans drawn in 1910. It was 52 by 16 feet in size and its freight room (directly behind the men in the picture) could be used to bunk the section crews maintaining track in the area. Unfortunately, the Stony Plain station no longer exists. Direct traffic control between dispatchers and train crews by radio, plus the suppression of rail passenger service to small communities, removed the need for most small depots in the West.

Grand Trunk Wharf at Prince Rupert, British Columbia

Above, an engineless mixed train sits beside the Grand Trunk Pacific's wharf in Prince Rupert, B.C., about 1913. Some men appear to be registering freight on the dock, while others gaze upon the stately craft in the harbour.

In June 1910, two GTP Coast Steamship Company ships inaugurated service between Prince Rupert and Vancouver, Victoria and Seattle. The parent Grand Trunk Railway, in eastern Canada had been anxious to expand to the west coast and compete with the Canadian Pacific.

Fort Simpson was originally chosen as western terminus of the new rail line but disputes with the U.S.A. over the Alaska-B.C. border at the turn of the century prompted Canadian Prime Minister Wilfred Laurier to order the GTP to change to a safer location, at the mouth of the Skeena River. It was to become Prince Rupert and it offered a shorter ship connection to the Orient than any other port in North America. The one summit on the land route to it, at the Yellowhead Pass (3,712 ft., or 1,114 m) gave grades no greater than those on the Prairies. Construction eastward from the port, to meet rails from the East, began in the Fall of 1908 but it was not until 7 April 1914 that the last spike was driven at Fort Fraser, near Vanderhoof, B.C.

The Fort Saskatchewan CNR Station

Above, *dolled up in bright, pure colors and a raven black roof, the Fort Saskatchewan, Alberta CNR station belies her age. It is the early 1970s and she has a long history, dating back to 1905, when Mackenzie & Mann's Canadian Northern Railway was built through here, on its way to Edmonton. Originally, her exterior was of wood and painted a rusty red. In 1911, a 30 foot addition to her freight room increased her length to 95 feet but it did little to improve her color. A coat of stucco in 1922 brightened things a little but it was not until the age of the diesel, about forty years later, that truly bright colors appeared on CNR stations. By that time, internal improvements had taken place as well. Gas heat replaced her coal furnace and stove in 1951 and electric light, running water and sewers were installed, in 1957.*

Upper Fraser Canyon, B.C.

At right, *a Canadian National freight cautiously threads its way down the Fraser at Skihist (near Lytton), British Columbia. It is 1977 and the harsh, rocky canyon is no less gentle than it was when the Canadian Northern Railway carved a narrow ledge for its trains 63 years before. The tunnels and slide sheds seen in the picture help to counteract the massive avalanches and boulders (some the size of boxcars) which Mother Nature periodically sends down.*

Canadian Northern's Last Spike was driven at Basque, a few miles away in the Thompson River Canyon, on 23 January 1915. Not quite three years later, on 20 December 1917, the financially exhausted railway was combined with the Canadian Government Railways, to form Canadian National Railways.

Refreshment at Edmonton, 1928

Above, *the enticing restaurant in the CNR Edmonton station of 1928 awaits patrons, shortly after opening. The revolving stools add both convenience and speedier service.*

Left: *The dignified exterior of the red brick edifice, whose pair of white Doric columns add a touch of classicism. All but the baggage-express section on the left was replaced in 1966.*

End of the Line, Vancouver, B.C.   *The CNR station's handsome, central archway became a gateway to the Canadian West's biggest city on 1 November, 1919. After VIA took over the CPR's passenger service in September 1978, all Vancouver trains terminated here.* **Below**, *VIA coaches on the maintenance sidings nearby. At left is the "Evanston," whose four staggered windows indicate duplex roomettes inside (the rest are bedrooms). Under the wooden shed are two ex-CPR stainless steel cars: a sleeper, and a domed observation containing bedrooms and two lounges.*

Groaners at Prince George

A pair of orange and black CNR diesels groan under the load, as they haul a heavy, 98-car coal train across the multiple trestles at Prince George, B.C. More units (out of the picture) push from further back. The loaded cars have been received from BC Rail and are now to be delivered to the Ridley Island coal terminal at Prince Rupert, 450 miles (720 km) to the West.

The chain of steel bridges over the Fraser River was built by the Grand Trunk Pacific, when its line came through, in 1914. Like the Canadian Northern, the GTPR quickly experienced financial difficulties and on 10 March 1919 it too was taken over by the federal government and made part of Canadian National Railways. The parent Grand Trunk followed in May of the next year. The war in Europe had been largely responsible but there was also a greater than expected slowness of development in the Canadian West in the years following construction of the two new transcontinentals.

Slugs at Calder

Two CNR diesel-electric hump yard units join forces at Calder Yards, Edmonton in August 1980. On the far right are the yard's control tower and a small diesel switcher.

Numbers 215 and 216 are General Motors 2,000 horsepower GP38-2 models, of 1973. They were converted in 1978 into "mothers" for the cut-down "children" (popularly known as "slugs") connected between them. The combination is also known as "master and slave," or "cow and calf" in some circles, the reason being that the low units have no control cab, nor do they have diesel motors and generators. They have only electric traction motors, to give added push to cars going up and over the hump in large freight yards. Commands and nourishment (electric power) are supplied by the full-sized "mother" units. The proper but plain name for slugs is "Hump Boosters" but hardly anyone uses it. The two in the above picture, CNR #275 and #278, were built by General Motors at the same time as #215 and #216 were converted to "mother" units, to handle the increasingly heavier freight cars of the modern world.

The Symington Hump Yards, Winnipeg

In the aerial view above, a single boxcar rolls downhill, past the control tower at lower right, headed for one of the sidings that branch out ahead. A locomotive, perhaps a Hump Unit and Booster like those seen on the preceding page, has given the car impetus by pushing it over a hump and now an operator in the tower selects and activates electric turnouts, to send it into the siding for its particular destination. Electronic sensors register the car's speed and electric wheel retarders grip the wheels just the right amount, so that the car does not run too fast and go crashing into other cars on the siding.

Sorting trains has ceased to be entirely reliant upon brakemen and hand-applied brakes. In days gone by, men had to ride the free-wheeling cars, hanging on for their lives and hoping to brake enough and not too much. A mistake could mean derailment, damage to a car or its merchandise. If too much brake was applied, the locomotive had to be called in to set the cars moving towards their siding again.

Saskatchewan Grain Car

SKPX 625041 is one of about a thousand similar covered hopper cars supplied by the Saskatchewan Government. The Canadian Wheat Board, the federal and the other prairie province governments provide another 14,000 such cars, to ship prairie grain to market. Each 59-foot car, with a capacity of 91,000 kg, carries some 3,000 bushels of wheat. That is about 50% more than boxcars. They are top loaded, bottom unloaded and like the one above are usually lined on the inside with epoxy and coated on the outside with vinyl. They have been a familiar sight on Canadian rails in the West, including the CNR, since the early 1970s.

Unloading Grain from a Boxcar

At a North Vancouver terminal elevator BC Rail's boxcar #4127, held by the couplers, is tipped to the side and rocked end to end, to empty its load of grain. Before 1920, when this hydraulic machinery was developed for the CNR elevator at Port Arthur, men used large shovels pulled by chains to clear out the grain.

CNR Wedge Type Snowplow

Canadian National's wedge snowplow #55379 rests in Calder Yards between storms, on a frosty January day in 1977. Its stove (as indicated by the stovepipe chimney near the back, with its horizontal downdraft controller on top) will likely soon be glowing with heat for the crew.

Amongst the plow's operating parts are steel wings (on which the wiggly CN Rail logo is placed). These can be opened laterally on each side, to push snow away from the track but they must be retracted when switch stands, bridges and other obstacles are encountered. A between-the-rails flap on the front must also be raised at level crossings, to avoid ripping up the roadway. Small, white flanger signs warn the plow operator where these precautions must be taken. The bright orange machine has no power of its own but relies instead on one or more pusher locomotives.

On the prairies, relatively little snow falls in places but high winds can whip it into tall, rock-hard drifts a kilometre (half mile) long, so wedges have plenty to do there. While snowfall through the mountains can be measured in metres and temperatures may fall to minus 30 degrees, the wedge type plow can often be very useful there too. Wedge plows, in fact, have been used everywhere in the Canadian Northwest, even in the normally mild coastal regions. Only where snowfall is extra heavy, or avalanches pile it up, are other machines needed.

CNR Rotary Snowplow

   CNR rotary snowplow #55361, shown above, is in retirement at the Canadian Railway Museum, near Montreal. Behind it is a fuel tender, for it is self-propelled and its boiler also produces steam for powering the huge, revolving blades at the front. Extra pushing power was normally added in the form of one or more locomotives, as suggested here.

   Rotary plows were generally employed only for the heaviest snow clearing tasks. Accumulations in the worst spots of the Northwest could total over 50 feet (about 15 metres). In extreme cases of deep avalanches, men with shovels sometimes had to reduce the depth first but otherwise little could stop the rotaries in their work. Rocks and trees hidden within the snow were about the only serious hazard to be faced.

   The rotary plow was a Canadian invention, originally devised by a Toronto dentist, J.W. Elliott and patented by him in 1869. His "compound revolving snow shovel" was ignored by railways, however, until perfected by Orange Jull, of Orangeville, Ontario. In 1883, Jull placed a knife wheel in front of the shovel wheel, to first chop up the snow. The whirling shovel then sent the white stuff spewing out a window in the casing. Produced by Jull and his associates in the United States, it soon proved itself on the Union Pacific, in Oregon. Canadian railways then saw fit to use the device and did so until the 1960s, when the bulldozer replaced it.

Vanished Glory - Canadian National Steam   **Above,** *CNR #2141, the last steam locomotive to run on Vancouver Island, on exhibition in a Kamloops, B.C. park, after retirement in August 1961. It was one of 25 built by the Canadian Locomotive Company at Kingston, Ontario in 1912, for the Canadian Northern Railway. During the 1920s to '40s over 300 of the 2-8-0 type operated in CN's Western Region, pulling both freight and passenger trains. Not surprisingly, CNR #2747, the first locomotive built in western Canada (in 1926, at Transcona) was indeed a 2-8-0.* **Below,** *CNR #6029 shortly after it left the erecting shops at Kingston, in July 1924. The powerful 4-8-2's eight 73-inch drivers gave fast acceleration, making it ideal for heavy passenger service. There were four of the U1b class working in the West by 1943, plus 20 Mountains of other classes. When the last regular CNR steam run in Canada was made on 4 September 1960, between Montreal and Ottawa, there was more than a little regret. Steam locomotives had a special sound, a special look and a special charm.*

RAILS INTO THE BUSH

Pacific Great Eastern's Locomotive #2

Engine #2 poses with a railway construction crew, as it works through the bush north of Squamish. Behind may be seen a drover caboose (an unusual combination baggage-passenger car with a cupola) lettered "Howe Sound & Northern Ry. Co." The Pacific Great Eastern took over the tiny HS&N and its equipment late in 1912.

The 2-6-2t had been built for the Howe Sound & Northern by Baldwin, in February 1910. Retaining its number on the PGER, it continued to haul supplies and logs until assigned in November 1913 to the North Vancouver-Whytecliffe line then being built. That job being finished the following summer, the rugged little saddletank began freight and passenger hauling. A head-on collision with gas railcar #103 on Labor Day 1916 sent #2 to Squamish once again, this time for rebuilding. Back in service, it remained on the PGE until 1920, when it was sold to the Comox Logging & Railway Company, on Vancouver Island. Having become obsolete by 1965, it was returned to the Pacific Great Eastern, put on display and preserved in Squamish, an honour accorded no other PGE steam locomotive.

Opening The Cariboo

Above, *northbound horse drawn freight wagons at Lillooet, c.1914. The gold rushes of the 1850s and '60s had failed to open the Cariboo country. Lillooet, at the southern end of the it, was reached by railway (from Squamish, on the Pacific, via Cheakamus Canyon and Anderson Lake), only in 1915.*

Left, *a wilderness survey camp for that railway, the Pacific Great Eastern, in 1913-14. Tents were for both living and working, their tables used equally for drafting or chess.*

Right, crews working with picks and shovels excavate earth to make a railway cut. A horse patiently waits for the four-wheel dolly to be filled, before drawing it away for dumping. Steam shovels were employed elsewhere on the PGE, to load cars with ballast, etc., but a great deal of work was done by hand.

Below, wooden ties drop into place from a Harris Tracklayer. Rails loaded on the flatcars behind will follow as soon as the ties are in place. The line has left the coastal forests and entered the dry, sometimes desertic inland region.

Timber Trestle Building

Left, a steam-driven piledriver mounted on a flatcar drives in vertical support poles, for a Pacific Great Eastern timber trestle bridge, in 1914.

The striking caribou herald used by the PGE from 1945 to 1965

Below, a work crew puts the finishing spikes into track on Bridge 120, a curved timber trestle on the PGE in the Lillooet region. Wherever possible, such structures were later filled in with earth, adding strength while eliminating the risk of fire.

PGE Steam **Above:** *Engine #52, built for the PGE by Montreal Locomotive Works in 1913 and scrapped in 1953. The 2-8-0 pulled the first regular Squamish-Lillooet passenger train, on 7 March 1915.* **Below:** *PGE #55 at D'Arcy, with the first passenger train from Clinton, in 1916. The 2-8-0 was built by CLC in Kingston, in 1914 and scrapped in 1954.*

North from Lillooet

 A long BC Rail freight winds northward, crossing the white steel trestle over the Fraser River above Lillooet, early in the summer of 1988. Scenery along the British Columbia Railway (formerly the Pacific Great Eastern) tends to be spectacular.

 Ownership of the PGE passed from the railway's builders, Foley, Welch & Stewart, to the Province of British Columbia, in 1918. Work from the line's end, in the bush north of Clinton (about 50 miles from Lillooet) was recommenced and by 1921 Quesnel was reached. Beyond that, some grading and bridge work was carried out but the objective, Prince George and a connection with the Grand Trunk Pacific (CNR) was not attained until 1952. For years, the press and public had jokingly referred to the PGE as the "Prince George Eventually." The North Vancouver to Squamish section, also long promised, was completed soon afterward, in 1956.

 Railway building above Prince George was much more rapid. The line to Chetwynd, Fort St. John and Dawson Creek opened in October 1958. Spurs to Mackenzie and Fort St. James followed in 1966 and 1968 respectively. A major, 250 mile (400 km) extension was then opened from Fort St. John to Fort Nelson in 1971, followed by a start the next year on one from Fort St. James towards Dease Lake. The railway now formed a giant "Y" almost the length of the province north to south. It had become the third largest railway in Canada, with roughly 1,400 miles of mainline track. Befittingly, it was renamed the British Columbia Railway, in 1972.

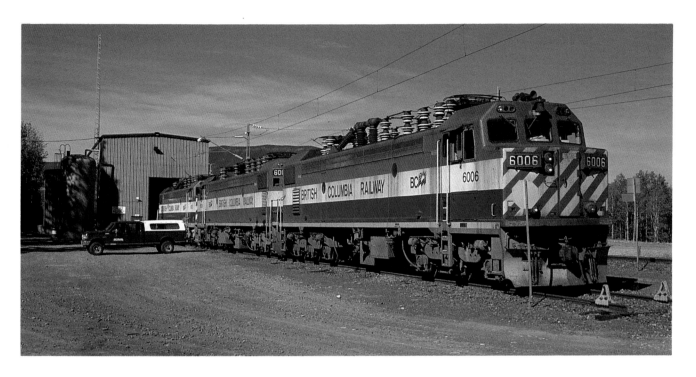

Electrics for Tumbler   **Above,** *three BC Rail 6,000 horsepower General Motors GF6-C all-electric locomotives at the maintenance sheds, in Tumbler Ridge.   Although the BCR completed dieselization in 1957, its Tumbler Ridge branch was built electrified, at 50,000 volts A.C.   The 82 mile (129 km) line to coal mines around Tumbler Ridge (opened on 1 November 1983) has four tunnels and long, heavy trains, two very good reasons for electric railroading.*

Greater Winnipeg Water District's Mack Railcar #31   This 1928 gas (now diesel) -electric railcar was bought second-hand in 1935, to help handle freight and passenger service on the 97 mile (155 km) railway to Indian Bay.   In the background is the St. Boniface terminal, built of red granite quarried along the GWWD right-of-way.   Main purpose of the short line is to maintain an aqueduct carrying Winnipeg's water supply.

Tunnel at White Pass

Locomotive #5, with flatcars and workers, approaches the White Pass & Yukon Railway's 250-foot tunnel 16 miles inland from Skagway, in the winter of 1898-99. The timber trestle on which the train rests was one of many needed to span the multitude of gaps in the sheer, granite cliffs. Over 30 men were killed during construction of this stretch of the WP&Y, some of them struck or buried by large chunks of rock loosened in blasting. Construction reached the summit of the pass (at Mile 20.4) on 18 February 1899.

The original line contained a treacherous switchback with 4% grades beyond this old tunnel and trains from Skagway had to back uphill across another timber trestle, to reach the summit. To overcome this dangerous obstacle, a steel cantilever bridge was built at Mile 18.6, in 1901. It in turn was replaced by yet another bridge and tunnel at Mile 18.8, in 1969.

The White Pass & Yukon was the second most northerly of Canada's railways. Only the 32-mile Klondike Mines Railway, running southeast from Dawson City to Sulphur Spring, was further north. When opened in 1906, the KMR bought two locomotives from the WP&Y, one of which was #5, shown above. It had originally been built by Baldwin in 1885, for the Columbia & Puget Sound Railway. After abandonment in 1913, KMR's #2 (ex-WP&Y #5) sat rusting until the early 1960s, when it and two other locomotives were placed on exhibition at Dawson City.

Shovelnoses at Whitehorse

    A string of four shovelnosed WP&Y diesel-electrics line up for fuel at the Whitehorse yards, in August 1982. A lone caboose waits near the two-stall engine house, on the left. They will soon be on their way to Skagway with a load of lead-zinc concentrate, perhaps some tank cars recently emptied of gasoline and aviation fuel, or flatcars with containers. All goods, even automobiles travelled in containers on the WP&Y, after 1955.

    The 36-inch narrow gauge locomotives were designed with shovel fronts in order to give them maximum ability to travel through deep snow and drifts. Regular plow pilots may also be seen mounted at the bottom. Eleven shovelnoses, numbered 90 to 100 were built by General Electric, in 1954, 1956, 1963 and 1966. They were 84 to 86 ton models and had 900 horsepower apiece. Two were damaged in a 1968 dive off a cliff but they were rebuilt and returned to service.

    The White Pass & Yukon Route's railway was connected to the outside world at Skagway by ships from North Vancouver and Seattle. At the Whitehorse end, there were Yukon river boats until 1955. From completion of the Alaska Highway during the Second World War (when the WP&Y was leased to the United States Government) there was also truck and bus transportation. Yukon road-building eventually brought about a decision in 1985 to abandon the railway.

Yukon Excursion Behind Number 73

    White Pass & Yukon's steam locomotive #73 chuffs southward with an excursion train to Skagway, Alaska, on 30 August 1982. The railway's undoing, the Skagway-Whitehorse highway, may be seen on the rugged Yukon hillside, just above the engine's white plume.

    The 2-8-2 was one of two built by Baldwin for the WP&Y in 1947. After dieselization was completed in mid-1964, they and two other identical Mikados of 1938 were retired. Number 73 sat on display at Bennett until 1979, when restoration for excursion service began. The other three locomotives were destroyed by a fire in the Skagway roundhouse, on 15 October 1969. Drive wheels on all of the locos were 44-inch diameter. Tractive effort was 25,200 pounds.

Steam at Carcross

Bearing white "extra" flags, WP&Y #72 pulls out of Carcross, southbound in 1982. The wooden trestle and swing bridge under the train are antiques of the original line.

Sternwheel river boats once plied the waters of the Yukon, stopping at Caribou Crossing (the town's first, unabbreviated name). Here supplies, passengers, mail and bags of ore could be transferred between boat and train. A general store and a three-storey hotel facing the railway station gave added convenience to travellers in the area.

It was at Carcross that the Last Spike of the White Pass & Yukon was driven, on 29 July 1900. From here it is 67 miles to Skagway and not quite 44 to Whitehorse, capital of the Yukon Territory. The railway was opened its full length on 15 August 1900.

Unlike the Pacific Great Eastern in British Columbia, which was built long after the gold rushes there had ceased, the WP&Y's builders hoped to exploit the Yukon's gold rush traffic. Started from Skagway in late May 1898, the railway was somewhat too late for that. Many gold seekers and their supplies were carried over the Pass to riverboats at Bennett in 1899 but by the time the railroad was completed to Whitehorse, the Rush was essentially over. The line came to rely upon ore shipments, supplies for the interior and in summer, tourists.

Of Life and Death

Above: *Northern Alberta Railways'* Muskeg Mixed, *ready to leave the Edmonton yards for the 299 mile trip to Waterways, in 1971. There will be an overnight stop at Lac La Biche, at mile 126.7. During the Second World War, there were trains daily but by the 1970s they had dwindled to twice a week, each way. The mixed trains, with freight cars in front and dark blue combination coaches at the rear, were for many years the only easy means by which mail, food, medicine and other supplies could be brought to those living in remote areas of the bush north of Edmonton. Roads were nonexistent in much of the region until after mid-century. The NAR was a lifeline as far as the Arctic. While rails ended at Waterways (Ft. McMurray) boats forwarded freight all the way down the Mackenzie River. A new rail line to Hay River in 1965 simplified and shortened the route. NAR mainline, which also went to Dawson Creek, totalled 925 miles.*

Opposite, Top Right: *Wreck near Castlegar, BC, about 1918. The smaller railways were not the only ones to operate through rough bush country. Like the NAR, the transcontinentals had to contend with track sagging into muskeg but in many areas of the mountains, they also had snow, mud and rock slides to master. Many crewmen still die in such accidents. Here, Canadian Pacific locomotive #664 has gone on the rocks and slid down to the water's edge. Apparently, it was not the end for the 4-6-0, however. It was scrapped only in 1947.*

Opposite, Bottom Right: *Derailment of a VIA train on the CNR mainline south of Blue River, BC, on 8 August 1980. A loose or broken rail is believed to have caused the accident. Because most passengers were in bed for the night, there were only some injuries, none were killed. Railways have always been the safest way to travel. Whereas Canada's worst rail disaster, at Beloeil, PQ, in 1864 killed only 83 people, an aircraft accident at Tenerife in 1977 killed 575. Road mishaps involve relatively few at a time but massacre thousands yearly.*

NAR Crane and Work Caboose

Northern Alberta Railways crane #16525 and its partner, work caboose #15508 rest at the NAR yards in North Edmonton, in 1972. They will soon be called upon to put trains back on the rails, for derailments are not uncommon on the line's long stretches of muskeg.

Water-laden earth is found almost everywhere along the rocky Canadian Shield, which stretches across the country's North in a broad arc. Lakes and swamps are plentiful too but are less treacherous than muskeg, for railway builders know in advance what they are facing. Muskegs may be a couple of hundred feet in depth, even though the surface appears reasonably solid, especially when frozen. The weight of track laid on muskeg is enough to make it sink and the passage of trains presses the roadbed even further into the earth. Rails quickly become uneven, causing wheels to derail and the only solution may be to add fill, perhaps piles and ballast until the sinking stops, which might not be for quite some time.

"Big Hooks" are also useful for railway construction work, to lift rail and entire switch assemblies. Early models were steam driven but the Brownhoist above has a diesel motor.

The Northern Alberta Railways was an assemblage of the Edmonton, Dunvegan & BC, the Alberta & Great Waterways and the Central Canada railways. They were all taken over by the Alberta Government in 1920 but the NAR was not incorporated until 1929, when it became the joint property of the Canadian Pacific and the Canadian National Railways. The CNR became sole owner in January 1981.

FEEDERS AND CONNECTORS

Burlington Northern Freight at Huntingdon

    Burlington Northern diesel-electric locomotives #2082 and #2075 arrive at the British Columbia border with a string of freight cars, in August 1983. The amber flasher on the cab roof of the green, white and black lead unit is a BN peculiarity.

    Burlington Northern is a 1970 amalgam of the Burlington Route, the Great Northern, the Northern Pacific, and the Spokane, Portland & Seattle railways. It does a brisk business with Canadian shippers at several points, from Blaine, Washington on the Pacific coast, all the way to International Falls, in northern Ontario. Forest products, potash, and sulphur fertilizers head the list of southbound freight, while manufactured goods and coke (from oil refineries on the Washington coast) are prominent items coming north.

    Most interchange of freight at Sumas/Huntingdon over the years has been with Burlington Northern (ex-Northern Pacific). It dates to the completion of a Canadian Pacific branch from the CPR mainline at Mission to Huntingdon, BC in May, 1891. At neighbouring Sumas, Washington it met rails of the Seattle, Lake Shore & Eastern (NPR) and the Bellingham Bay & BC (Milwaukee Road) whose lines arrived there from Bellingham, that same year. Another interchange was made possible in 1909-10, when the Fraser Valley line of the BC Electric (since 1988 the Southern Railway of BC) was built south from Abbotsford to the border. Until March 1980, when the Milwaukee Road's western lines were abandoned, four operating railway stations crowded into the two, tiny border hamlets.

Left, *a buggy and an open electric trolley, its running boards brimming with male passengers, meet on muddy Main Street, in early 1895. Behind, stands the Northern Pacific Railway's massive Winnipeg station-hotel. It was considered the finest west of Montreal, until it went up in flames one cold February night, in 1899. Fire hoses froze as the fine, chateau-style structure was reduced to ashes.*

The NPR had big plans for expansion in Manitoba, when it built this monument, in 1892. After completing a mainline from the lakehead to Portland in 1883, NPR turned attention northward. Financial problems stalled expansion however, and by 1910, its network of lines in Manitoba had disappeared into the hands of either the Canadian Northern, or the Great Northern railways.

Top Right, Opposite Page: *Victoria & Sidney Railway's locomotive #1, a diamond stack 2-6-0, arrives in Sidney (Vancouver Island), having just completed the 20-mile trip from Victoria, via Royal Oak, the west shore of Elk Lake, Keating and Saanichton. An unusual feature of the V&S was that it used no dispatcher, only verbal messages between crews by telephone.*

The railway carried cordwood, lumber, farm products and mail. Opened in 1894, it provided a fast route to the Gulf Islands but unable to make a profit, it was sold to the Great Northern Railway, in October 1902. The GNR had no more success and the line closed, on 30 April 1919.

Bottom Right, Opposite Page: *In a snow-filled landscape, GN #471 approaches the Centre Star Gulch trestle at Rossland, BC, with a train of ore cars for the Le Roi mine's loader, about 1910. The locomotive's squared, Belpaire firebox was a distinguishing feature of GNR steam.*

The Great Northern arrived in Rossland through a takeover of Daniel Corbin's Red Mountain Railway, in July 1898. Corbin's line had reached Rossland from Northport, Washington, in December 1896. Service continued until July 1921, by which time the mines were in decline.

Great Northern In British Columbia

Amtrak at White Rock

Amtrak's gleaming Pacific International *rolls swiftly through White Rock, BC on a fine autumn morning in 1979. Passengers will enjoy a splendid, relaxing view along the coast from the high, bi-level coaches. The train has left Vancouver at 6:50 a.m. and diesel-electric locomotive #218 will have it into Seattle, 156 miles to the south, by 11:20.*

Great Northern's shoreline route through White Rock opened in 1909, replacing the more steeply graded line from Blaine through Cloverdale to New Westminster, opened in February 1891. The White Rock station was a customs & immigration point and people could be held there under lock and key, if their papers were not in order. Passenger business to the small village itself was light, except in summer, when a Camper's Special was run.

Passenger service on the Seattle-Vancouver run was heavy in the days of steam and 12-car trains were normal. After new highways lured away passengers, patronage dropped and by 1969 service was cut to one train a day. It was suspended altogether, in April 1971. Amtrak (formed in January 1970) decided to try once more in 1975 but passenger trains were again discontinued on 30 September 1981. Burlington Northern continued to operate freights on the line, however. Coal trains need it to reach the Roberts Bank terminal and important interchange is made with Canadian National Railways and BC Rail in New Westminster and Vancouver.

Union Pacific Interchange at Eastport, Idaho

    Shiny red CP Rail diesels rub shoulders with canary yellow growlers of the Union Pacific, as interchange is made at Kingsgate/Eastport, in September 1987. Only freight moves through this point to-day but earlier in the century luxurious, high speed CPR passenger trains passed on their way to Spokane and Portland.

    The line from the border to Spokane, Washington was built by Daniel Corbin, with funds advanced by the Canadian Pacific. It was announced in January 1905 and by mid-1907 the 141.8-mile Spokane International Railway was complete. On 1 July 1907, the Spokane Flyer *and the* Soo Express *began running between Minneapolis-St. Paul and Spokane (see also page 22). The CPR's trains were even able to continue on to Portland, using Oregon Railway & Navigation Company (Union Pacific) trackage. The CPR's new route was shorter overall than the Great Northern's and shortly afterward the Canadian Pacific was awarded a contract to carry the United States mails. This was one more volley in the feud between the CPR and the GN, over rail supremacy in southeastern British Columbia. The Great Northern had gained control of Corbin's Spokane Falls & Northern, from Spokane to Northport, Washington and his Nelson & Fort Sheppard Railway, from there to Nelson, in 1898 (see also page 58). Competition between the Canadian Pacific and the Great Northern was fierce for years afterward.*

Ore Train at the Mother Lode Mine

Canadian Pacific locomotive #952 prepares to leave the Mother Lode Mine with ore cars for the nearby smelter in Greenwood, BC. A second, unidentified locomotive sits to the left, close to the loading silo, probably waiting with empty cars. The date is 1903 and production at the mine is in full swing.

Prospectors discovered the mine in 1891 but it was not until a New York group built a smelter at Greenwood, that the mine came to life. The BC Copper Company began production of copper, gold and silver in 1901, fed mainly by the Mother Lode mine. Over 400 men worked at the smelter alone, changing Greenwood from a patch of wilderness into a fair-sized town, with substantial brick buildings on its streets. Copper prices rose as the Allies stockpiled metals but when the war ended in 1918, prices fell and many copper mines closed, including the Mother Lode in 1918 and the Granby, at Phoenix, in 1919. With the mines went the smelters and the towns did not rebound until the 1950s.

To handle the heavy ore trains, the CPR considered electrification of the Greenwood to Nelson section of its Kettle Valley route, plus parts of its mainline through the about-to-be-built Connaught Tunnel in Rogers Pass, in 1908. Electricity was to come from the Bonnington Falls power station near Nelson but CPR electrification, after endless studies, remained only a dream.

Ore Concentrate at North Vancouver

Above, a modern industrial scene at Vancouver Wharves, in North Vancouver. A Heede cover crane moving on its own, very broad gauge rails has gone along the string of cars at left, picking off their covers and laying them neatly beside the tracks. The cars are now to be moved by a switch engine to an unloader, where the lead and zinc concentrate will be removed and placed in weather-proof storage sheds, pending transfer to ships at the wharf. The empty gondolas will then be moved back to the crane, to have their covers replaced, before returning to the concentrator. Although some shipments arrive by truck and container, the majority of the million or more tonnes of concentrate handled at this facility each year is moved by rail.

Covers for the gondola cars are of steel or fibreglass and may be in sections, each weighing over a ton. Car capacity varies between 80 and 100 tons (72 to 91 tonnes).

Vancouver Wharves Railway locomotive #25, seen to the right of the crane with an empty car, is an 80 ton General Electric diesel, built in 1947. It's history goes back to a beginning as the National Harbours Board locomotive #1, then Canadian National #74 until 1966, when it was acquired by Vancouver Wharves Limited. The steeplecab is ideal for switching, for its driver has to move very little each time the train changes direction, which is every few minutes.

British Columbia Electric Railway Interurban at New Westminster

BC Electric's #1212 poses with its crew on a New Westminster street, about 1918. The smartly-dressed motorman and conductor in their neat, dark blue uniforms exude an air of dependability. Note that while BC Electric interurbans used city streetcar tracks in town, they followed private rights-of-way between cities, to gain time.

The wood-bodied interurban coach had been built in 1908, in the company's New Westminster shops. It is now showing signs of age. The leather strap safety fender on the front must have seen better days and all that is left of the original, roof-mounted destination board is a pair of mounting brackets. A "12" on the dashboard is almost effaced and the original name of the car, the "Abbotsford," also appears to be missing from the side panel.

Beside the front door, an oval sign informs passengers that this is a Central Park car. The Central Park was the first of three BCER lines connecting New Westminster and Vancouver. Built by the predecessor Westminster & Vancouver Tramway Company, it opened in 1891. The Canadian Pacific's line from Marpole (south Vancouver) was leased in 1909 and a Burnaby Lake route was built in 1911. While the latter was abandoned in 1953 and the Marpole line returned to the CPR in 1986, the Central Park line right-of-way remains. It is now shared by the Southern Railway of BC and BC Transit's Skytrain.

BCER Interurban Coach Interior

   The handsome interior of BC Electric #1307, an interurban trailer. It was built in BCER's New Westminster shops, in 1913 and boasts 42 cool, rattan seats, a non-slip ribbed floor, luggage racks (for the interurbans ran from Vancouver all the way to Chilliwack, over 80 miles away) graceful arched windows and an arched roof. Cords over the aisle, on either side of the electric lamps, transmit start signals between conductor and motorman. A smoking compartment lies at the far end, separated from the rest of the coach by a glass-panelled door.

   The number of interurban lines in the Canadian West was limited to the BC Electric on the mainland and the Saanich Peninsula of Vancouver Island, the Winnipeg, Selkirk & Lake Winnipeg in Manitoba, the Edmonton Interurban and the Lacombe & Blindman Valley Railway, in Alberta. BC Electric, the last survivor, ceased passenger operation in 1958. Governments, unfortunately, lacked the foresight to upgrade and expand interurbans into commuter rail lines.

Comox Logging Train

A logging train of the Comox & Campbell Lake Tramway Company pulls out of a Comox area camp with a full load, about 1910. The railway was re-named the Comox Logging & Railway Company that year, after being absorbed by the Canadian Western Lumber Co. Note that the 2-6-2 rod engine is burning wood for fuel and requires a large spark arrester on its smokestack. Coal being less incendiary, it was used later. In 1954, the railway here closed and equipment was moved to the company's other Vancouver Island operation, at Nanaimo Lakes.

Logging companies began using steam donkeys (stationary steam engines with winches and a mile or so of cable), in the late 19th century. Logs were hauled out of the forest along board skid roads. When the timber got to be too far away, the practice of laying rails on each side of these skid roads for small steam locomotives developed. Proper railroads, such as that shown above (built in 1909) followed and logs were then carried on cars, some of which consisted only of two trucks held together by the logs themselves. Light, 40 pound rail was often laid on the bare ground, without ballast, because most of the line was temporary and had to be moved as timber was used up. Grades of 10% and very sharp curves were not uncommon. All these characteristics, plus the casual operation (at least one lokie is remembered to have run with the driver's leg hanging out the window) gave logging railways a memorable, very special aura.

Dumping Logs, Haney

Logs hit the water with a splash at Haney, on the Fraser River east of Vancouver, c.1925. Locomotive #99, of the Abernethy & Lougheed Logging Company has brought carloads of logs from the surrounding hills and stands clear while they are dumped into the water. Note that one rail of the unloader is higher than the other, to ease the operation. The logs will be floated downstream to lumber, pulp and paper mills.

The locomotive is a Climax type, with canted cylinders driving a main wheel not touching the rails. Motion is transferred to an internal drive shaft and thence to the small wheels of the two supporting trucks via gears. This arrangement added tractive ability and improved performance on the crude track and sharp curves so common to logging railways. Abernethy & Lougheed had seven steam locomotives, six of which were of the geared type.

The A&L line, begun in 1919, grew to be 85 miles (136 km) in length, the largest of its kind in western Canada. Arterial lines ran at the base of the Golden Ears mountains, with short spur lines branching into the remote timber. The railway was of standard gauge and had a connection to the Canadian Pacific at Kanaka Creek, to receive boxcars of supplies and to run locomotives down to Vancouver for overhaul. The operation closed in late 1931 but not before receiving the visit of none other than Winston Churchill and his son, Randolph.

Loading Wood Chips

A high-sided CP Rail gondola receives its fill of wood chips at a sawmill near Craigellachie, British Columbia. Fans blow chips from the saw area up a metal tube and through a hollow arm swinging like a pendulum to each end of the car. A rusty-colored hood has been lowered onto the car to prevent spillage. After filling, the car will be delivered to a factory using chips for pulp, or other fibre products.

By the 1980s, the forest industry had all but dispensed with railway logging, as seen on the preceding pages. Closure of Crown Forest Industries' Nanaimo Lakes line out of Ladysmith in 1986 left the Canadian Forest Products railway at Englewood, in northeastern Vancouver Island the lone survivor. Motor trucks, which began to be used in the 1920s, eventually proved more economical than railways for short hauls. Nevertheless, forest products in the late 20th century accounted for the largest part of railway revenues in western Canada. Lumber was the top gross earner for the CNR, which had over 11,000 boxcars to carry it. Canadian National was also shipping 50,000 carloads of wood pulp per year to paper mills at the end of the 1980s and two-thirds of gross revenue on BC Rail was coming from the transport of forest products. Thus, despite the forest industry's wholesale shift to motor trucks for some purposes, it has, like the mining industry, remained a great user and feeder of railways.

RAILWAYS FOR CITIES

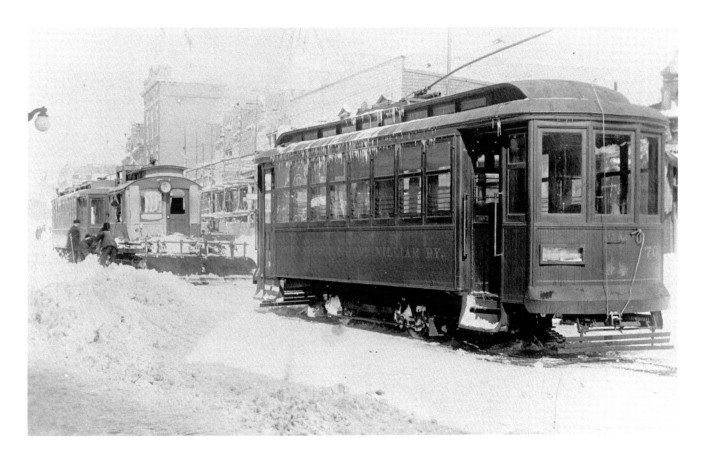

Snowtime at the Lakehead

   Port Arthur & Fort William Electric Railway's #70 waits while men and a sweeper struggle to clear a path in the snow for an oncoming tram. Date of the photograph is unknown but the name on the letterboard, plus the presence of Life Guard fenders suggest it is not much before 31 December 1913, when the Fort William, Ontario system began to operate on its own.

   Life Guard fenders appeared shortly before the war of 1914, replacing the scoop type that protruded from the front of earlier models (see Winnipeg's #458 on next page). As we see on #70, the Life Guard was confined under the bumper, eliminating some accidents that were caused by the older fenders themselves. When bumped, the bar at the front causes a scoop further back, under the car, to drop onto the rails.

   Almost all horsecars in Canada had to be converted to sleighs in winter but with the arrival of electric trolleys, near the end of the 19th century, that changed. Canada's first electric street railway, at Windsor, Ontario (opened 3 June 1886) reverted to sleighs the first winter but from the early 1890s, when electric sweepers were introduced by the Ottawa Car Company and others, Canada's streetcars were able to run year round.

   Electric railways brought many benefits to city dwellers. Service to distant and hilly areas became feasible. Travel time was decreased and there were economies in energy and space requirements. Add the non-polluting factor and the sum becomes ideal urban transportation.

Winnipeg #458 Loading Passengers   People scurry to board a Portage Avenue streetcar, in early July 1949. Boarding is by the rear door only. Exit is by the front only, where the motorman (seen in the centre window) takes fares and controls the car.

Car #458 was built by the Winnipeg Electric Railway Company itself, in 1911. It was converted to PAYE (Pay As You Enter) operation in 1914 but rebuilt into a "Front Exit" car in 1930. Winnipeg had resisted one-man operation until 1924, objections having come from patrons fearing for their safety and unionized crewmen fearing for their jobs. Other cities had adopted it much earlier. Calgary, for instance, had one-man operation by 1917.

Interior of Winnipeg Streetcar #360

A lone passenger sits relaxed, at the rear of spacious Winnipeg tram #360, on a late August day in 1950. Comfort could not be much better at home. Wire grille may be noted outside the windows on the right, the side facing passing traffic. Windows on streetcars were almost always openable and accidents could occur when passengers stuck heads or arms out of them.

Like #458, Car #360 was company-built but in 1909. Both had 44 seats, double trucks, and a length of 33 feet (9.9 metres).

As we can see, this car is one-man operated by this time. In two-man cars, a conductor was generally at the back and gathered fares. When the doors were clear, he gave the motorman a "go" signal, with a double tug on the bell cord. In PAYE operation, a system invented in Montreal in 1905, the conductor was able to remain constantly on the rear platform. The motorman was freed of distractions and better able to do the driving. With the introduction of one-man operation, the motorman became burdened with fare collecting and had to rely on mirrors to determine when to start the vehicle, a system perhaps not quite so safe. Clanging of the bell was often retained, to signal all and sundry that the car was about to move.

Calgary Streetcar #14

A replica of Calgary Municipal Railway's #14 begins the trip from the gate to the main display area at Calgary, Alberta's Heritage Park. On the left in this September 1991 view, the front of Canadian Pacific's preserved Selkirk #5931 (a 2-10-4) can also be seen.

The original car #14 was built for CMR by Ottawa Car Company in 1910, a year after the system was put into operation. The wooden, monitor-roofed car was 46½ ft. long, had 44 seats and Brill 27G trucks. It was made for Pay As You Enter but was converted to one-man operation in 1917, increasing seating to 54 in the process. After the Calgary system was closed, on 29 December 1950, car #14 sat outside for several years. By the time it was moved to Heritage Park, it was both decayed and incomplete. Drawings, photographs and an old car used as a summer cottage provided information for the replica body. Seat frames of the original #14 were covered with new cane and the original body frame was given trucks, motors and operating equipment from two ex-Toronto sweepers. The park's trolley system was opened on 5 April 1975.

The peculiar door seen in the picture above, replacing the right-hand front window, was specifically designed to enable the motorman to better see passengers boarding. It opened outwardly, using a hand crank mechanism. The invention was the brainchild of the railway's superintendent, T.H. McCauley. Although widely used in Calgary, it was rare elsewhere.

Nelson Car #23 On The Wharf Loop

On a sunny June day in 1994, Nelson's restored Car #23 rounds the City Wharf loop, at the foot of Hall Street. The roughly one-mile line from Lakeside Park and the open shelter at which Car #23 stops are almost new, having opened just two years earlier.

The Nelson trolley is mainly for pleasure riding, unlike the former city tram system, that provided basic urban transportation from 31 July 1899 to 20 June 1949. The old line was not much bigger, however. With only 2.1 miles (3.3 km) of track, it was the smallest streetcar system in the British Empire.

Car #23 was built in 1906 for the Cleveland, Ohio system and came to Nelson second-hand, in 1924. Nelson already had two operating cars but needed a spare. After tram service was terminated in 1949, the car became a change room at a skating rink. Several winters later, it was moved over to the North shore, to serve as a dog kennel and eventually as a storage shed. In 1982, the Nelson Chamber of Commerce took an interest in the by-then historic piece and a restoration project was launched. Volunteers and students at Selkirk College worked on it until 1987, when it was turned over to the Nelson Electric Tramway Society. Parts were donated by the Toronto Transit Commission, Cominco in Trail and BC Transit in Vancouver. When the British Columbia Government provided a $433,000 grant, the line became a reality.

Sprinkler On Yates Street, Victoria

    British Columbia Electric's S52 sprinkles unpaved Yates Street in the dawn hours, attempting to lay the dust before the heat of another hot summer day begins in earnest. The date is circa 1908, a year after the company had built the twenty-foot sprinkler. Crews inevitably consisted of at least two men: one to drive, one to dispense the water. On larger sprinklers (also called "flushers") there might also be a third member to help refill the tank from fire hydrants, or to pacify nervous horses nearby.

    Sprinkling roads was one more valuable and welcome service rendered to city dwellers by electric street railways in Canada. If it were a private company operating under franchise from the City, there was often a clause in the contract requiring the service, either free, or for a fixed sum. As well as laying dust and cooling streets in summer, sprinklers helped sanitation by flushing away the dirt left by the multitude of horses in use up to mid-century. Both bread and dairy products were delivered daily by horsedrawn wagon and there were many private carriages. Motor vehicles were expensive to buy and not very reliable, before the early 1930s and in addition, paved roads outside the downtown core were not too common much before that time. The economic Depression of the 1930s and the Second World War retarded considerably the general changeover to motor vehicles in Canada, until after 1945.

Vancouver Streetcars On West Hastings Street, May 1939

Streetcars rumble down West Hastings Street in Vancouver BC, on a balmy day in May, 1939. It is Royal Visit time and Union Jacks, a few Canadian Ensigns and a lone Stars & Stripes flutter gaily from store facades. It is a brief moment of joy, as the King and Queen traverse the country stirring support and patriotism, before the conflict almost everyone knows must come begins.

Streetcars themselves would be used heavily during the war, as they had been twenty-five years before. They would both provide transportation and act as mobile billboards, advertising for recruits and government bonds. They would be invaluable in a country short of oil, auto parts, tires and new vehicles. Workers would rely on them and servicemen in training, or on leave would find the electric railways indispensable. The streetcars of Canada would carry well over a billion passengers in 1945 alone, over 200 million more than were carried in 1920, when twice as many systems existed.

The war was not kind to the electric railways. Although revenues climbed dramatically in those years, equipment was worn out by war's end. Added to the effects of the great depression of the 1930s, most streetcars were outdated and dilapidated by 1945. The youngest of the trams in this picture, #270, was built in 1913. As soon as they were available, Canadians rushed to buy new automobiles and by 1965, only Toronto's streetcars remained.

Scott Road Skytrain Station, Surrey, B.C.

Diesel BC Transit buses interchange passengers with the Vancouver Skytrain, at the Scott Road station. It is March 1992, just two years after a new, 2,033-foot (616 m) bridge over the Fraser had brought service to Surrey. For the moment, this is the eastern end of the system but by late 1994, four more stops would be added, taking the line southward to an intersection with King George Highway, deep within the municipality.

The new, light rapid transit system opened in January 1986, from downtown Vancouver to New Westminster. It quickly attracted riders and within four years had carried a hundred million passengers. Public transit is both needed and wanted in modern day urban society and when it is fast, clean, safe, comfortable, economical and frequent, it can be highly successful.

The Vancouver Regional system is fully automated, its trains driverless except in emergencies and severe weather. Control is normally by computer at a central command centre in New Westminster. The cars have linear induction motors, which pull themselves along a broad, central rail magnetically. Most of the line is elevated on concrete uprights, as seen in the picture above but there is also a short stretch at ground level in the middle of the system, plus subway at the western, downtown Vancouver end. Designer of the system was the Urban Transportation Development Corporation, in Ontario.

The Light Rapid Transit Bridge In Edmonton

An Edmonton Transit System train crosses the North Saskatchewan River, southbound on the new LRT bridge, in mid-July, 1994. It has just emerged from the subway under the downtown area and now heads for the University of Alberta campus, whose buildings can be seen on the right. At the far end of the bridge, the line curves and plunges into tunnel leading to the underground University Station. Under the bridge's double-tracked main deck is slung a pedestrian and bicycle path, whose spiral approach ramp can be seen by the roadway.

The Dudley B. Menzies LRT Bridge is 1,980 feet (600 m) long and 75 feet (23 m) above the river. It was started in October, 1988 and finished by summer 1991, but was not immediately opened to traffic, for the University station was not ready until August, 1992.

The bridge's construction is of singular interest. It was built of 216 precast concrete segments, erected by cantilevering them off the piers. Each box girder segment was laced to the next, until a total of 152 miles (253 km) of steel cable were consumed.

Edmonton was the first city in Canada to build a modern, Light Rapid Transit line. Construction began in September 1974 and the first section, from Central Station 4½ miles north to Belvedere, was completed in April, 1978. Subsequent additions from both ends brought total mileage to 8 miles (12.8 km) by 1992 and more were planned.

Edmonton Duewag LRT Cars At The New Shops

Articulated unit 1031 parks outside the new maintenance shops, built in 1988 near the Edmonton system's northern terminus. On the left in this 1989 photo, a southbound train of two double units passes on the mainline, headed for Corona Station, then the southern terminus.

Edmonton's LRT cars are Siemens Duewag U2 models, descendants of those first introduced on the Frankfurt, Germany system, in 1968. Calgary also chose the same type for its new system, as did San Diego, St. Louis, Denver, Sacramento, Portland and Pittsburgh later, in the United States. Some of these cars were equipped with low-entry doors, some with high-entry doors (as we see in the Edmonton unit above) and still others with a combination of the two.

Edmonton and Calgary systems utilize only high, floor-level station platforms. These provide the maximum in rider convenience and safety. Problems arise, however, when they are placed along city streets, for young passengers may be tempted to jump down to ground level, upon leaving the trains. Proper stations with regulated access are best where high platforms are used.

The U2s have welded steel bodies and can only be operated in married pairs, since they are hinged together and share a central bogie. Their wheels have rubber inserts, for quiet operation and electronic anti-slip devices sense slippage and automatically decrease the power supply. Operating current is 600 volts DC and maximum speed is 50 miles per hour (80 km/hr).

Calgary LRT Car Interior

    This interior view of a Calgary Duewag U2 car reveals how very comfortable rapid transit riding can be. The unit is air-conditioned, well lit, has rubber, anti-slip flooring and seats are upholstered with warm, sturdy wool fabric. Stainless steel upright poles provide steady support for standing passengers and they are easily kept clean. In the centre of the car may be seen the flush, circular floor panel that moves with the bogie below. Note that there is no impediment to movement throughout the double unit. For safety, doors have pressure-sensitive edge strips to detect the presence of human bodies passing through. They normally reopen but some cases of individuals trying to force themselves through after the doors have closed have brought tragic results. Capacity of the cars is 64 seated, with 98 standee spaces.

    With city road traffic already hopelessly congested and acres of valuable urban space wasted on parking lots and freeways, a great increase in electric railways both within and around cities appears inevitable. Canadians in the great Northwest were fortunate to have three excellent systems by the 1990s and considerable expansion must surely come in the 21st century.

Photo Credits

The photographs in this book are either the author's, or reproduced through the courtesy of the following:

BC Archives & Records Service, Victoria: pages 59t (#49894), 74 (#E-7597)
British Columbia Railway: pages 43-47
BC Transit: pages 64, 65
Canadian National: pages 38 (#48877), 42b (#23126),
Canadian Pacific: pages 7 (#1960), 8 (#19991), 12t (#18170), 15t (#17), 15b (#12755), 19b (#795), 27
    (E1865-1)
Foster M. Palmer: pages 70, 71
Glenbow Museum Archives, Calgary: pages 21b (#NC 2-257), 22 (#NA 1313-8)
Manitoba Archives: page 58
Nanaimo & District Museum Society: page 26
Provincial Archives of Alberta, E. Brown Collection: pages 18t (#B2626), 30 (#B598)
Public Archives of Canada: page 14 (#C5303)
Rossland Historical Museum Association: page 59b
Thunder Bay Historical Society: page 69
University of Washington, E.A. Hegg Collection: page 50
Vancouver Public Library: pages 10 (#678), 11 (#7770), 12b (#1797), 31 (#49919), 55t (#1764), 62
    (#1782), 66 (#6044), 67 (#5803), 75 (#7883)
Western Development Museum, Moose Jaw: page 18b

Some Useful Bibliography

Berton, Pierre, The National Dream (the CPR to 1881), *Toronto: McClelland & Stewart, 1970.*
_____, The Last Spike (the CPR 1881-1885), *ibid.*
Bytown Railway Society, Trackside Guide, *Ottawa: Bytown, 1984, etc.*
Clegg, A. and Corley, R., Canadian National Steam Power, *Montreal: Trains & Trolleys, 1969.*
Ewert, Henry, Story of the BC Electric, *North Vancouver: White Cap, 1986.*
Hart, E.J., The Selling of Canada: The CPR and the Beginnings of Tourism, *Banff: Altitude, 1983.*
Hearn, G. and Wilkie, D., The Cordwood Limited, *Victoria: BC Railway Historical Association, 1976.*
Hind, Patrick O., Pacific Great Eastern Steam Locomotives, *Victoria: BCRHA, 1984.*
Kelly, Brian, Transit in British Columbia, *Madiera park: Harbour, 1990.*
Lamb, W. Kaye, History of the Canadian Pacific, *New York: Macmillan, 1977.*
Lavallee, Omer, Canadian Pacific Steam Locomotives, *Toronto: Railfare, 1985.*
_____, Narrow Gauge Railways of Canada, *Montreal: Railfare, 1972.*
Martin, J. Edward, On a Streak of Lightning: Electric Railways in Canada, *Harrison: Studio E, 1994.*
_____, Railway Stations of Western Canada, *Harrison Hot Springs, BC: Studio E, 1980.*
_____, Western Canada's Railways, *White Rock, BC: Studio E, 1986.*
McDonald, J.D., Railways of Rossland, *Rossland Historical Museum Association, 1991.*
Moore, George A., "Manitoba's Railways," *Canadian Rail, July and October 1975 issues.*
Regehr, T.D., The Canadian Northern Railway, *Toronto: Macmillan, 1976.*
Sanford, Barrie, McCulloch's Wonder, Story of the Kettle Valley Railway, *Vancouver: Whitecap, 1977.*
Taylor, G.W., History of Mining in British Columbia, *Saanichton: Hancock, 1978.*
Turner, Robert D., Vancouver Island Railroads, *San Marino: Golden West, 1973.*